MAGIC SCIENCE

Peter Eldin
Illustrated by Stuart Trotter

Hippo Books
Scholastic Children's Books
London

Scholastic Children's Books,
Scholastic Publications Ltd,
7–9 Pratt Street, London NW1 0AE, UK

Scholastic Inc.,
730 Broadway, New York, NY 10003, USA

Scholastic Canada Ltd,
123 Newkirk Road, Richmond Hill,
Ontario, Canada L4C 3G5

Ashton Scholastic Pty Ltd,
P O Box 579, Gosford, New South Wales,
Australia

Ashton Scholastic Ltd,
Private Bag 1, Penrose, Auckland,
New Zealand

First published by Scholastic Publications Limited, 1992
Text copyright © Peter Eldin, 1992
Illustrations copyright © Stuart Trotter, 1992

ISBN 0 590 55011 X
Printed in Spain

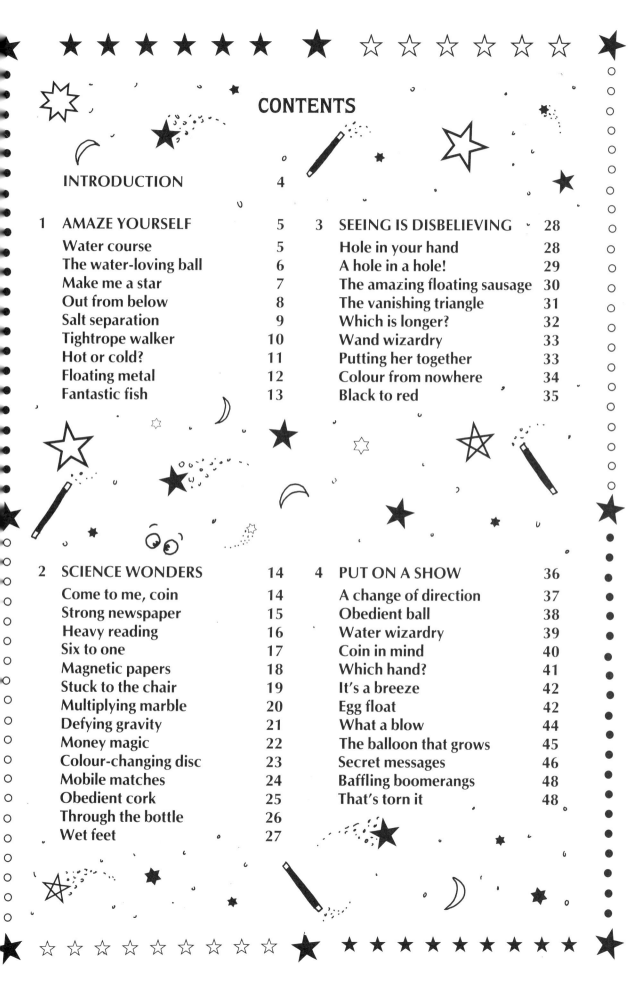

CONTENTS

INTRODUCTION

MAGIC SCIENCE will enable you to do some amazing tricks. But they are rather different tricks from the sort you will find in most books about conjuring. You don't have to be a magician to do them! This is because the tricks in this book are not based on magicians' principles – they are based on the principles used by scientists. Although everything in MAGIC SCIENCE has a magical appearance, each trick is really a scientific experiment.

With MAGIC SCIENCE you will be able to give everyone the impression that you are a great magician. Really you are a great scientist.

Science is not a boring, subject as many people think, it can be really exciting. You don't need any special apparatus to try the tricks. Everything you need can be found around the house or in the book itself. So, what are you waiting for? Start reading, and you can begin to amaze your friends with MAGIC SCIENCE.

Remember to practise each trick carefully two or three times before you perform it in front of anyone.

1
AMAZE YOURSELF

Science is such an amazing subject, you'll find you can even amaze yourself when you try out the tricks in this section. Of course, that doesn't mean that you can't show them to anyone else! But try them out for you own enjoyment first, and then amaze your friends.

WATER COURSE

With your amazing magical powers you can bend a stream of water!

Apparatus
a comb
a water tap

The trick
1 Run the tap very slowly to produce a thin, even stream of water.
2 Pull the comb through your hair a few times.

Magic Science
This trick is done by *static electricity* (see pp. 9 & 38). When you pull the comb through your hair it becomes electrified. Holding the comb near the water attracts the water just as a magnet attracts pins. Don't let the water touch the comb or the trick will not work.

3 Hold the comb near the running water as you say the magic word "Abracadabra".
4 The water bends towards the comb!

THE WATER-LOVING BALL

When you suspend a ping-pong ball near a stream of running water, you would expect the water to push it away. Instead the opposite happens.

Apparatus

a ping-pong ball
a water tap
piece of sticky tape
some cotton

The trick

1 Tape one end of the cotton to the ball.
2 Hold the other end of the cotton and allow the ball to hang near the running tap.
3 The ball seems to be attracted to the water.

Magic Science

This is an example of "Bernoulli's law" (see p. 18). This means that there is a lower pressure in the running water than in the air surrounding it. Because the *air pressure* (see pp. 15, 26, 27, 39 & 44) is greater, it pushes the ball into the water. This law was discovered by Daniel Bernoulli over two hundred years ago.

THE FACT THAT MOVING AIR HAS A LOWER PRESSURE THAN STILL AIR IS ANOTHER EXAMPLE OF BERNOUILLI'S LAW.
THE LAW APPLIES TO GASES AS WELL AS TO LIQUIDS.

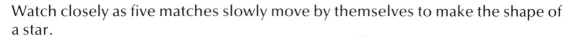

MAKE ME A STAR

Watch closely as five matches slowly move by themselves to make the shape of a star.

Apparatus
five used safety matches or toothpicks
a smooth surface
a wet sponge

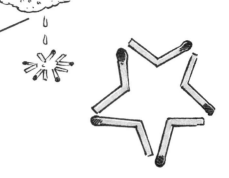

The trick
1 Break the matches at their centres.
2 Don't break them completely in two.
3 Arrange them on a smooth surface in the shape shown in this drawing:

4 Squeeze the wet sponge over the matches, so that a drop of water falls on the centre of each match.
5 The matches will slowly move by themselves to form the star shape shown in the second picture.

Magic Science
Wood, like all plants, has lots of fine tubes in it. When the water falls onto the matches, these tubes suck up the water and start to swell. This is called *capillary action*, and the swelling forces the matches to open out into a star shape.

It's a fact
The Ancient Egyptians used this idea to split stones when they were building the Great Pyramids. They bored holes in any large rocks they wanted to split. Then they put pieces of wood into the holes. When water was poured onto the wood it swelled up so much that the rocks would split!

OUT FROM BELOW

Stack eight pieces from a checkers game up in a pile. Then amaze yourself by taking out the bottom checker without touching any of the others or causing the stack to fall over!

Apparatus
eight checkers pieces
a ruler

The trick
1 Stack the checkers pieces in a pile on a table that has no cloth on it.
2 Now try to remove the bottom piece without touching any of the others and without causing the stack to fall. Can you do it? Of course you can't!
3 To make the trick work, take your ruler and hit the bottom piece with a quick, smart blow of the ruler.
4 The bottom piece will be knocked out but the rest of the stack will remain together!

Magic Science
All objects resist movement until they are forced to move. This resistance is called *inertia*. You knock out the bottom piece but inertia holds the others together in one pile.

Here's another example of inertia:

1 Balance a playing card on the forefinger and middle finger of your left hand.
2 Balance a coin on top of the card and over your fingers.
3 Now whip the card away with the thumb and forefinger of your right hand. The coin should stay on your fingers!

SALT SEPARATION

Mix a little salt and pepper together. Now separate them using just a comb!

Apparatus
salt
pepper
comb
woollen cloth

The trick
1 Mix a small amount of salt and pepper together.
2 Rub your comb briskly with the woollen cloth.
3 Hold the comb near the salt and pepper mixture.
4 The pepper jumps up from the mixture and onto the comb!

Magic Science
Static electricity (see pp. 5 & 38) in the comb (formed by rubbing the comb with the cloth) attracts the lighter grains of pepper. The heavier grains of salt remain.

It's a fact
All experiments that make use of static electricity work best in dry weather. This is because electricity short-circuits or discharges itself when it comes into contact with water, and therefore it no longer works.

It's a fact
Static electricity is sometimes called "frictional electricity", because it is created when things are rubbed together.

The English scientist William Gilbert was the first person to study static electricity properly. He even showed Queen Elizabeth I some amazing tricks, like this one. Because of his experiments he is often called "the Father of Electricity".

TIGHTROPE WALKER

Make a toothpick or used safety match balance on a piece of string!

Apparatus

a used safety match or toothpick
a cork
two forks
some string
an adult to help you

The trick

1 Ask an adult to cut a V shape in one end of the match.
2 Push the other end of the match into the cork.
3 Push the forks into each side of the cork.
4 Tie one end of the string to a door handle or bedpost and hold the other end in your hand.
5 Place the notched end of the match on the string.
6 You may have to adjust the position of the forks, but eventually you will be able to balance the match on the string as shown in the picture.

Magic Science

This trick works because of something called the *centre of gravity*. The centre of gravity is the central point of the object, over which the whole of its weight is evenly balanced. Normally a cork wouldn't balance on the string but by attaching the forks to the cork its centre of gravity is lowered to make this impossible balance possible.

centre of gravity

HOT OR COLD?

You'll really be confused when you try this trick. It makes a bowl of warm water feel both hot *and* cold at the same time!

Apparatus

a bowl of cold water
a bowl of luke warm water
a bowl of hot water (not so hot that you cannot put your hand in it)

The trick

1 Put your right hand into the bowl of hot water and your left hand in the bowl of cold water.
2 Leave your hands in the water for a little while.
3 Now place both hands in the luke warm water.
4 The water will feel cold to the right hand but hot to the left hand!

Magic Science

The water feels cold to the right hand because it has got used to the higher temperature of the hot water. It feels warm to the left hand because that has adjusted to the cold water.

FLOATING METAL

Does metal sink or float in water? It sinks of course! Or does it? Try this trick and find out.

Apparatus

a bowl of water
a needle (or pin)
a small piece of paper
two forks

The trick

1 Take your needle and rub it slowly between your hands. Be careful not to stick it into your skin – when you do this, it hurts!
2 Place the needle on the piece of paper.
3 Float the paper on the surface of the water.
4 Very slowly and gently push the paper under the water with the forks on either side.
5 The needle remains floating on the water.

Magic Science

Water is actually made up of tiny particles called *molecules*. Because these molecules attract one another, they cling together to form a sort of skin on the surface of the water. The scientific term for this is *surface tension*.

When you rub the needle between your hands you cover it in a thin layer of grease. As grease and water repel each other the weight of the needle is supported by the surface tension of the water, which gives the needle a waterproof cushion on which it can float.

THIS TRICK WILL ONLY WORK IF THE NEEDLE IS COMPLETELY DRY TO START WITH.

FANTASTIC FISH

You can make a cardboard fish swim in a bowl of water!

Apparatus

the fish shape from the cardboard
   section in the middle of this
   book
washing-up liquid
a bowl of water
a drinking straw

The trick

1 Cut out the fish shape.
2 Cut out the red portion so that
   you have a hole in the centre of
   the fish and a narrow opening
   from the centre to the tail.
3 Place the fish on the surface of
   the water. Do this carefully so
   that the upper surface of the fish
   does not get wet.
4 Dip one end of the drinking
   straw into the washing-up
   liquid.

5 Put your finger over the top end
   of the straw and remove the
   straw from the bottle.
6 Put the end of the straw over the
   hole in the centre of the fish.
7 Remove your finger from the
   end of the straw. This will allow
   the washing-up liquid to drip
   from the straw and onto the
   surface of the water.
8 The fish will begin to move
   forward across the surface of the
   water.

Magic Science

The washing-up liquid is heavier
than the water. When you drop the
liquid into the hole in the fish it
starts to spread out in a flat layer
across the surface of the water. As
the cardboard stops it, the liquid flows
down the narrow channel toward
the tail of the fish.

It's a fact
The fish in this trick moves in
accordance with one of the *laws of
motion* described by Sir Isaac
Newton in 1687. This law says that
for every action there is an opposite
and equal reaction. This means
that as the washing-up liquid is
forced out of the tail of the fish,
the fish itself is forced forwards.

2
SCIENCE WONDERS

The word "science" comes from the Latin word "scire" which means "to know". All scientists are trying to find out why things happen the way they do, so they carry out experiments just like the ones in this section. If you want to discover some of the wonders of science for yourself, try these experiments.

COME TO ME COIN
Magically you can make a coin creep towards you when you call it!

Apparatus
a glass tumbler
two large coins
one small coin (this must be
    thinner than the large coins)
a table with a cloth on it

Come to me Coin!

The trick
1 Put the three coins in a row on the table, the small coin between the other two.
2 Turn the tumbler upside down and rest it on the two larger coins as shown.
3 Bet someone that they cannot get the smaller coin out from beneath the glass without touching any of the coins or the glass.
4 When your friend gives up you say "Come to me, coin!" as you repeatedly scratch the tablecloth a short distance from the glass.

5 The small coin begins to creep towards you from under the glass!

Magic Science
Each time you scratch the cloth, the material is pulled towards you a little and this brings the coin as well. When you move your finger for the next scratch, the threads of the material spring back into place, but because of *inertia* (see p. 8) the coin stays where it is. So, each scratch brings the coin a little nearer to you. Keep scratching and it will eventually come out from beneath the glass.

STRONG NEWSPAPER

Try out this trick and you can prove that an ordinary newspaper is stronger than your strongest friend!

Apparatus
a long ruler
a sheet of newspaper

The trick
1 Place the ruler on a table so that it sticks out over the edge of the table.

2 Open out the newspaper and put it flat on top of the ruler.
3 Ask a friend to hit the projecting end of the ruler as hard as possible so that the newspaper is forced into the air.

4 No matter how hard your friend hits the ruler the newspaper does not move.

Magic Science
Air pressure (pp. 6, 26, 27, 39 & 44) pushing down on the paper stops it from moving. Air pressure is about one kilogram on every square centimetre of the newspaper. A newspaper that measures about 30 cms by 45 cms covers an area of 1350 square centimetres. Multiply that by one kilogram per square centimetre and you will see that your friend is trying to lift a weight of about 1350 kgs!

IF YOU USE A WOODEN RULER FOR THIS TRICK YOU ARE MORE LIKELY TO BREAK THE RULER THAN TO LIFT THE NEWSPAPER!

HEAVY READING

Your strongest friend is really in trouble now. You're going to make him so weak he won't even be able to lift a book!

Apparatus
a heavy book
two metres of strong string

The trick
1 Tie the string around the book.
2 Ask your strongest friend to take one end of the string in each hand.
3 Now challenge your friend to pull the string out straight, lifting the book up at the same time.
4 No matter how hard your friend tries he will not be able to pull the string straight, and so be able to lift the book.

Magic Science
When your friend's hands are close together holding the string it will not take much effort to move them apart. But as the angle of the two halves of the string gets bigger, a much greater force is needed to lift the book. So, the harder your friend tries to get the string straight, the more impossible the task becomes!

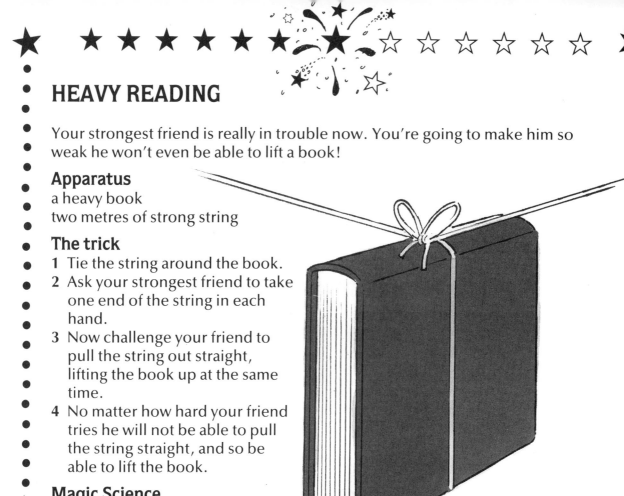

SIX TO ONE

Of course, you are stronger than all your friends and you can prove it with this trick!

Apparatus
a wall
six other people

The trick

1 Stand facing the wall.
2 Place your hands flat against the wall.
3 Ask the first person to stand behind you and put his hands on your shoulders.
4 The other people then stand one behind the other, each with their hands on the shoulders of the person in front.

5 Now ask everyone to push hard to see if their combined strength can push you against the wall.
6 No matter how hard they push, you will not be crushed against the wall. So you see, you are stronger than six people!

Magic Science

You are not really stronger than all the people pushing against you. In fact each person is only pushing against the strength of the person in front. That person is naturally pushing back to prevent himself collapsing. So the only person who is pushing against you is the one next to you.

MAGNETIC PAPERS

When a friend tries to blow two strips of paper apart, they move towards one another!

Apparatus

two strips of paper about 3 cm by 30 cm

The trick

1 Hold the strips of paper sideways on, one in each hand, at one end.
2 The papers should be about 8 cm apart.
3 Ask a friend to blow between the papers so that they move further apart.
4 No matter how hard your friend blows, the papers will only move towards each other.

Magic Science

If the speed of air is increased, its pressure goes down. Blowing lowers the air pressure between the papers. The normal air pressure on the outsides of the paper is now greater than the pressure on the inside, so the papers are pushed inwards.

It's a fact
Bernoulli's law (see p. 6) is one of the most important principles that enable airplanes to fly.

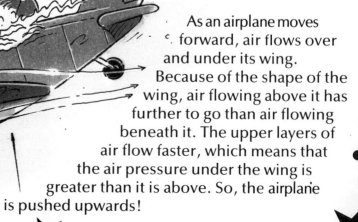

As an airplane moves forward, air flows over and under its wing. Because of the shape of the wing, air flowing above it has further to go than air flowing beneath it. The upper layers of air flow faster, which means that the air pressure under the wing is greater than it is above. So, the airplane is pushed upwards!

STUCK TO THE CHAIR

Touch someone on the forehead and they are suddenly stuck to their chair!

Apparatus
a chair (without arms)
a friend

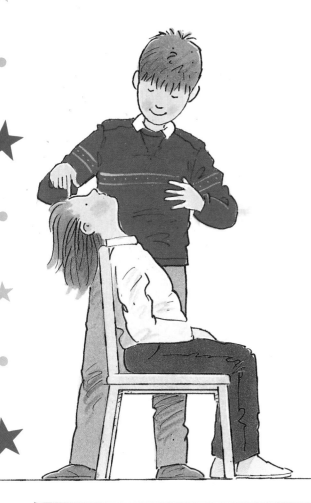

The trick
1 Ask your friend to sit on the chair.
2 Get her to put her hands on her legs, her feet flat on the floor and to tilt her head back as far as possible.
3 Place one of your forefingers on her forehead and press down slightly.
4 Now challenge your friend to get up out of the chair without using her hands.
5 She just cannot do it!

Magic Science
When someone gets out of a chair they lean forward. This alters their *centre of gravity* (see p. 10) so that the legs can lift the body upwards. With the head back, the centre of gravity is changed and it is impossible to get up if there are no arms on the chair to give added support.

MULTIPLYING MARBLE

One marble seems to turn into two marbles!

Apparatus
a small marble

The trick

1 Place the marble on a table.
2 Touch each side of the marble between the first and second fingers of your right hand.
3 You will feel one marble – what else did you expect?

4 Now cross your first and second fingers.
5 Close your eyes.
6 Place your crossed fingers against the marble and roll it back and forth on the table.
7 Can you now feel two marbles?

Crossing the fingers tricks the brain into believing there are two marbles.

It's a fact
This trick is known as *Aristotle's Illusion* after the Greek philosopher who lived 2,300 years ago! He was one of the first people to write about how the brain works.

DEFYING GRAVITY

No one will believe their eyes as they watch a paper cone defy the laws of gravity and roll up hill!

Apparatus
two books (or boxes) of different sizes
two smooth sticks
cartridge paper
sticky tape
scissors

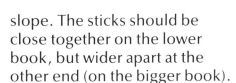

The trick
1 Cut two pieces of paper, each about 15 cm by 10 cm.
2 Fold each piece into a cone and tape the two sides together.
3 Tape the two cones together carefully using small pieces of tape. The trick may not work if the cones are buckled in any way.
4 Lean the two sticks across the two books to form a gentle slope. The sticks should be close together on the lower book, but wider apart at the other end (on the bigger book).
5 Place the cone on the sticks near the bottom of the slope.
6 Make mystic passes over the cone with your hands as it rolls up the sticks.

Magic Science
Look at the drawing above and you will see that the centre of the cone (which is its centre of gravity, see p. 10) actually lowers as it moves up the sticks, because it is obeying the law of gravity. So, although the cone appears to be moving up hill it is actually moving down hill.

> *It's a fact*
> The great English scientist, Isaac Newton, wrote about the *law of gravity* in 1685. According to tradition, he first began thinking about gravity when an apple fell from a tree onto his head. In truth he worked out his ideas by studying the behaviour of the sun and the planets.

MONEY MAGIC

Now you see it, now you don't! You can make a coin vanish and then come back again!

Apparatus
a coin
a cup
some water
a friend to help

The trick
1 Put the coin into the bottom of the cup.
2 Pour some water into the cup, so that it is only half full.
3 Look at the coin.
4 Keep looking at the coin as you move away slowly.
5 Suddenly, the coin will disappear!
6 Stay in the same place and ask your friend to pour some more water slowly and gently into the cup.
7 The coin will now reappear before your very eyes!

Magic Science
When light rays pass in or out of water they bend slightly because light travels more slowly in water than in air. This bending of light is called *refraction*. Place a spoon in a glass of water and look at it from the side. Because of refraction the spoon appears to bend where it enters the water.

It's a fact
Because of refraction ponds and rivers look shallower than they really are. Never believe what your eyes can see – the water is a lot deeper than it looks.

COLOUR-CHANGING DISC

Spin the disc of many colours and watch as the colours all turn white!

Apparatus

disc A from the card section in the
   middle of this book
a pencil
scissors

The trick

1 Cut out the coloured disc.
2 Push the point of a pencil
  through the centre of the disc to
  make a spinning top.

3 Spin the top and the colours on
  the disc will appear to change
  into white.
4 When the top slows down, the
  colours come back!

Magic Science

Daylight is really a mixture of different colours. When the disc is spinning we
see all the colours at once, so the disc appears to be white.

It's a fact

Sir Isaac Newton was the first
person to discover that daylight is
made up of different colours.

   He darkened a room so that just
one small ray of sunshine was
coming in through the window. He
then placed a *prism* (a triangular
block of glass) in the ray of
sunlight. As the light passed
through the prism it showed all the
colours of the rainbow.

It's a fact
A rainbow is formed by sunlight
passing through raindrops. Each
drop is rather like Newton's prism
and it splits the sun's light into
different colours.

MOBILE MATCHES

Astound your friends when matches, floating in a glass of water, move apart at your command.

Apparatus
two used safety matches
a glass of water
a paper drinking straw
a piece of soap

The trick
1 Before showing anyone this trick, secretly push one end of the straw into the soap.
2 Wipe off any soap that sticks to the outside of the straw so that the straw looks quite normal.
3 Float the matches on the surface of the water.
4 Position them so they are floating slightly apart.
5 Touch the surface of the water in the centre of the floating matches with the secretly soaped end of the straw. Be careful not to touch the matches when you do this.
6 The matches will float apart.

Magic Science
The soap weakens the surface tension of the water (see pp. 12 & 25) and the matches are pushed apart, as they are attracted more strongly to the molecules in the water which haven't been weakened.

Now move them back together again!

Apparatus
two used safety matches
a glass of water
a paper drinking straw
some sugar

The trick
1 Before showing this trick to anyone, secretly dip one end of the straw in the sugar.
2 Wipe off any sugar that sticks to the outside of the straw.
3 Float the matches on the surface of the water.
4 Move them so that they are a short distance apart.
5 Dip the secretly sugared end of the straw into the water, between the two matches.
6 The matches will float slowly towards the sugar.

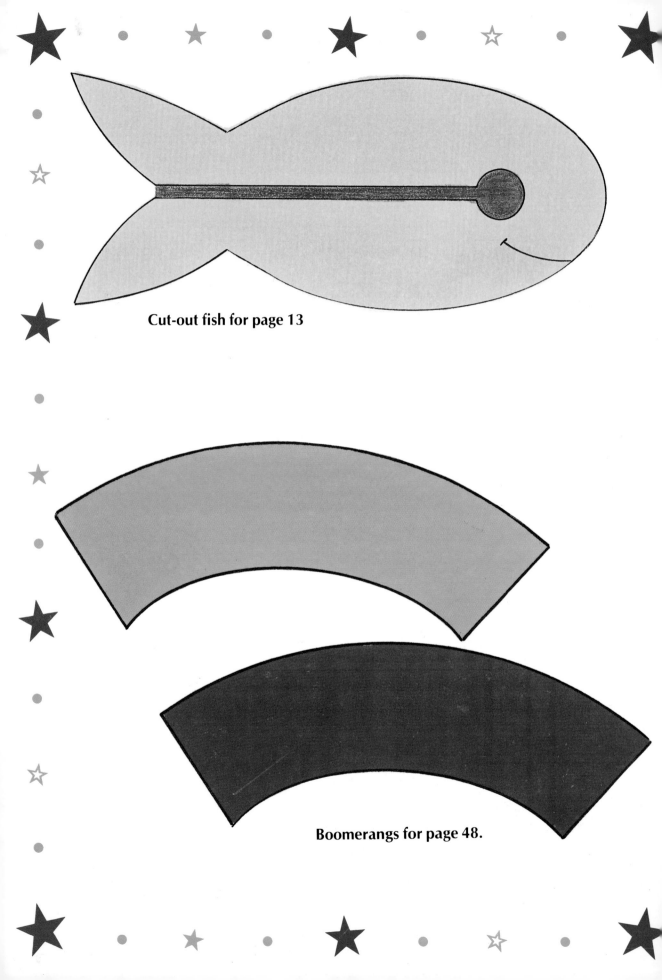

Cut-out fish for page 13

Boomerangs for page 48.

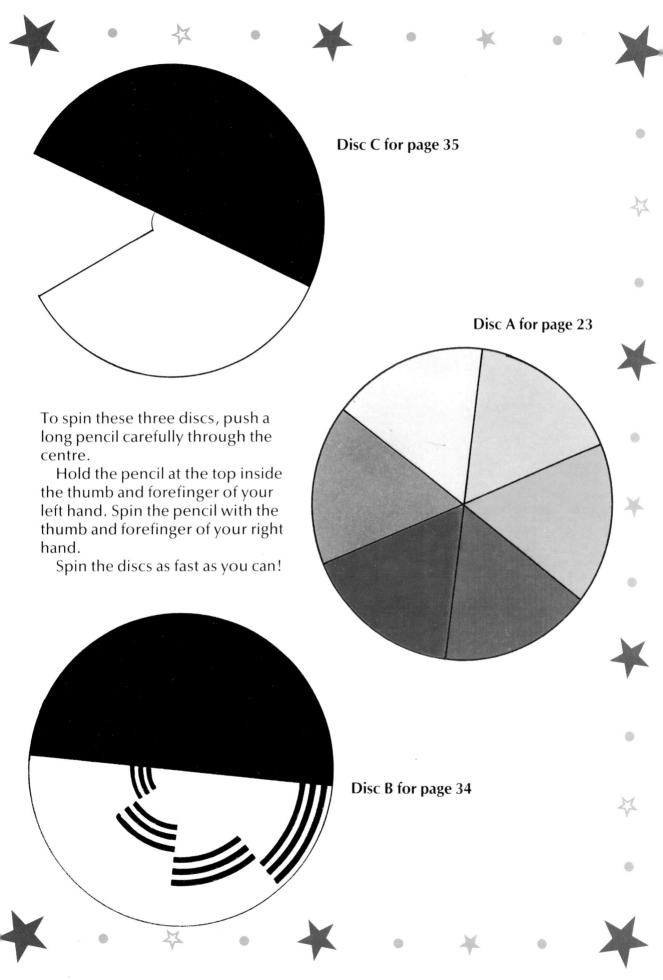

Disc C for page 35

Disc A for page 23

To spin these three discs, push a
long pencil carefully through the
centre.

Hold the pencil at the top inside
the thumb and forefinger of your
left hand. Spin the pencil with the
thumb and forefinger of your right
hand.

Spin the discs as fast as you can!

Disc B for page 34

Magic Science
As the sugar dissolves, it sucks in water. This creates a current on the surface which pulls the matches towards the centre.

A good idea
If you dip one end of the straw into soap and the other end in sugar you can combine both these tricks. But make sure no one is watching when you turn the straw around!

OBEDIENT CORK
Challenge your friends to position a cork in a tumbler of water, so that it floats in the middle of the surface. They won't be able to do it, but you can show them how!

Apparatus
a glass tumbler
a cork
water

The trick
1 Give a friend a glass of water and a cork.
2 Ask her to put the cork in the water so that it floats in the centre.
3 Your friend won't be able to do it – the cork will float to the side of the glass.
4 You now pour some more water into the glass. Do this slowly and steadily until the glass is filled

right up to the brim.
5 The cork will now be floating in the middle of the water's surface.

Magic Science
Because of surface tension (see pp. 12 & 24) the water molecules are attracted to the sides of the glass, and push the cork away from the middle. If you look through the side of the glass the surface of the water looks like this: and is called the *meniscus*.

When the glass is filled to the top the water molecules have nothing to cling to, but the surface tension holds them together. The meniscus is now higher in the centre than it is near the rim of the glass so the cork floats to the highest point.

THROUGH THE BOTTLE

Your breath is so strong you can force it through the glass of a bottle!

Apparatus
a bottle
a candle
plenty of puff

The trick
1 Ask an adult to light the candle and stand it safely on a table.
2 Place the bottle on the table, close to the candle.
3 Boast that your breath is so strong you can force it through the glass to blow out the candle.
4 Blow hard at the bottle.
5 The candle will go out!

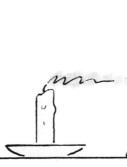

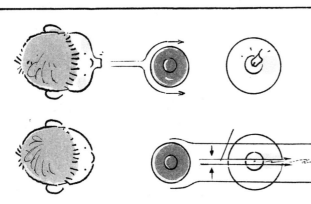

Magic Science
Your breath doesn't really go *through* the bottle, it goes around it. The air flows round both sides of the bottle. The fast-flowing air causes the air pressure (see pp. 6, 15, 27 & 39) in between to lower. As soon as you stop blowing, air rushes into the area of low pressure and this gush blows out the candle.

WET FEET

Trick your friend with this special bottle and she'll end up with wet feet!

Apparatus

a plastic bottle with a screw cap
a nail or pin
a friend with a good sense of
　　humour

The trick

1 Use the nail to make several
small holes in the bottom of the
bottle. Ask an adult to help you.

2 Remove the cap and put the
bottle in a bowl of water.

3 When the bottle is full of water,
screw the cap back on. You
must put the cap on while the
bottle is still under the water.

4 Take the bottle out of the water
and wipe it dry. Be careful not to
squeeze the bottle as you dry it,
or some of the water will be
squeezed out.

5 Hand the bottle to a thirsty
friend. When she unscrews the
cap, water will pour out of the
holes in the bottom of the
bottle.

HEH! HEH! HEH!

6 Run away as fast as you can!

Magic Science

While the cap is on air pressure (see pp. 6, 15, 26 & 39) pushes up on the base of
the bottle and stops the water from coming out. When the cap is removed,
the air pressure on the top of the water is the same as that on the bottom, and
the water is pushed out through the holes.

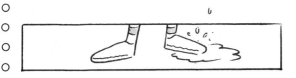

3
SEEING IS DISBELIEVING

Sight is our most important sense. And yet our brains often fool us into seeing things that don't exist. Look at the tricks on the following pages and you may never believe your eyes again!

HOLE IN YOUR HAND

When you do this trick you'll really believe there's a hole in the side of your hand!

Apparatus
a tube of paper or cardboard

The trick

1 Hold the tube in your right hand and look through it with your right eye.

2 Hold your left hand a few centimetres in front of your left eye.
3 With both eyes open you will see a large hole in the side of your left hand!

Magic Science
Our left and right eyes see slightly different images. The brain puts these two images together. When you look through the tube, the right eye sees the hole; the left eye sees your left hand. Your brain puts these two pictures together, and it appears there is a hole in the side of your left hand!

A HOLE IN A HOLE!

Look through the centre of a card and you can see a hole within a hole!

Apparatus
a postcard
a cardboard tube (about 10 cm
   long)

The trick

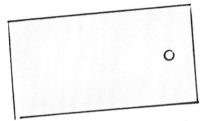

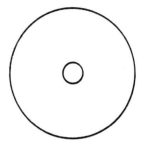

1 Make a small hole in the
   postcard. It should be about
   halfway down the card and
   approximately 1 cm from the
   right edge.

4 Look through the tube and at
   the card at the same time.
5 You will see a hole in the card
   (as you did in your hand on page
   28) but there is also a small hole
   in the centre of the large hole!

2 Hold the postcard about 6 cm in
   front of your right eye.
3 Hold the tube against your left
   eye.

Magic Science
This is caused by two different
images (one from each eye) being
seen together. See page 28.

OUR EYES SEE EVERYTHING
UPSIDE DOWN. OUR BRAINS
TURN WHAT WE SEE THE
RIGHT WAY ROUND!

THE AMAZING FLOATING SAUSAGE

With your two magic fingers you can make a sausage appear that floats on air!

Apparatus
a pair of eyes
two fingers

The trick

1 Place the tips of your two forefingers together.
2 Hold the two fingers up in front of your eyes.
3 Look beyond your fingers to something else a short distance away.
4 Now move your fingers very slightly apart.
5 There will appear to be a sausage floating between your fingers!
6 Don't look directly at your fingers or the sausage will disappear!

Magic Science

Because your eyes are looking at something further away than your fingers, the image of your fingers is seen separately by each eye. The two images overlap to make the sausage-like shape.

THE VANISHING TRIANGLE

Make a triangle disappear.

Apparatus
this book
three small coins, counters or
  buttons

The trick
1 Ask someone to look at the
  picture on this page.
2 Draw their attention to the white
  triangle between the three black
  spots.
3 Place a coin on each of the black
  spots.
4 The triangle has disappeared.

Magic Science
The triangle disappears because it
never existed in the first place! If
you look carefully at the drawing
you will see that there are no lines
drawn to make the triangle! It is
simply an *optical illusion*
(something that tricks the eyes).

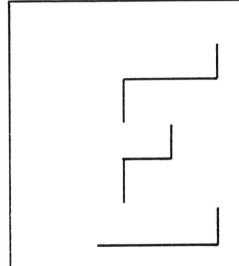

It's a fact
Our brains often trick us into
believing we see things when
there is really nothing there. Take
a look at the shape on this page. It
looks like a letter E. Now turn the
page to one side and you will see
that it doesn't look anything like a
letter E at all. It is simply a few
unconnected lines!

WHICH IS LONGER?

Ask a friend to point to the longer of two lines. Whichever one he chooses he will be wrong.

Apparatus
this book
a ruler

The trick

 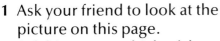

1 Ask your friend to look at the picture on this page.
2 Ask him to say which of the two lines is the longer.
3 He is very likely to say that the top line is the longer of the two.
4 Now hand him a ruler and ask him to measure them.
5 He will discover they are both the same length.

Magic Science
It is a simple optical illusion. The top line looks longer because the fins at each end draw the eyes outwards. The arrows on the bottom line draw the eyes inwards and the line looks shorter.

STAND BACK AND LOOK AT THE LINES RUNNING ACROSS THE PAGE. ARE THEY PARALLEL? MEASURE THEM AND YOU WILL SEE THAT THEY ARE. THE ANGLES OF THE LINES RUNNING DOWN DISTRACT YOUR EYES, JUST AS THE FISH DO IN THE TOP PICTURE.

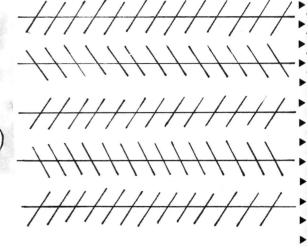

WAND WIZARDRY

Ask a friend to pick the longer of two magic wands but she'll get it wrong!

Apparatus
this book
a ruler

The trick
1 Show your friend the picture of two wands on this page.
2 Ask her to pick the longer wand.
3 It is very likely that she will pick wand B.
4 Get her to measure the wands with a ruler and she will find they are both the same length.

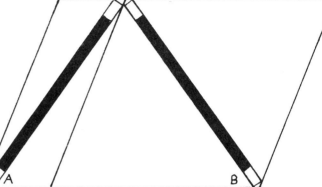

Magic Science
The shapes around the wands trick the brain into seeing one wand as longer than the other.

PUTTING HER TOGETHER

You've heard of magicians who saw people in half? Well, you can put someone together again.

Apparatus
the picture on this page

The trick
1 Look at the picture of the professor, which is drawn in two pieces.
2 Slowly bring the page towards your eyes.
3 The two halves will move towards each other.

Magic Science
From a distance your eyes see the two halves of the professor as separate. As you come closer to the page the two images overlap into one.

COLOUR FROM NOWHERE

Spin a black and white disc and make lines of colour!

Apparatus
disc B from the cardboard section in the
    middle of this book
a pencil

The trick
1 Push the pencil through the
   centre of the disc to make a
   spinning top.
2 Spin the disk like a top.
3 Spin it one way and the outer
   lines seem to be red and the
   inner lines blue.
4 Spin it the other way and the
   outer lines seem to be blue and
   the inner lines red!

Magic Science
As the lines spin the *optic nerve*,
which connects the eye to the
brain, sends your brain confusing
messages. In an effort to sort out
these strange messages, the brain
creates colours that it thinks are
correct.

It's a fact
This disc is known as "Benham's
Colour Top" after the English
writer Charles E. Benham who
invented it about a hundred years
ago.

BLACK TO RED

When this disc spins over a printed page it makes the black print turn red!

Apparatus
disc C from the cardboard section in the middle of this book
a pencil
a book, magazine, or newspaper

The trick
1 Push the pencil through the centre of the disc to make a spinning top.
2 Place the top you have just made on a black and white page of a newspaper, book or magazine.
3 Spin the disc like a top.
4 When you look through the gap in the disc, the print on the page takes on a reddish hue. This works best with the disc close to the print.

Magic Science
The appearance of colour is caused in the same way that colour appears using "Benham's Colour Top", described on page 34. It is the brain's attempt to make sense of the confusing messages it is receiving from the eye.

It's a fact
Experiments aren't usually bad for you, but Sir Francis Bacon died as a result of an experiment he tried in March 1626. It had snowed, and he wondered if ice would stop meat rotting. He bought a chicken and stuffed it full of snow. We now use freezers to preserve all types of food but, unfortunately for Sir Francis, he caught a chill and died three weeks later.

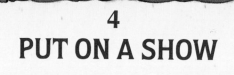

4
PUT ON A SHOW

The tricks in this section are especially effective if you want to put on a small magic show. But don't try to learn all of them at once. Just pick about four and practise them again and again, until you are sure you can make them work every time.

Your audience will soon get fed up if you have to stop for any reason halfway through a trick, so make sure you always have everything ready before you start your show.

Even the simplest tricks can be amazing as long as you perform them well, but do be careful not to let out your secret as this can really spoil the surprise.

One of the most important rules of magic is *misdirection*. This is when you draw people's attention away from your trick. For example, pretending to be a mind-reader for *Coin in mind* (page 40) draws your audience's attention away from the real secret of the trick. Before you perform a difficult trick, try to think up a few simple phrases you can say to misdirect your audience's attention at the vital moment!

A CHANGE OF DIRECTION

- Make an arrow change direction without touching it!

Apparatus
- a piece of cardboard (approximately 15 cm × 12 cm)
  a pencil (or crayon)
  a glass tumbler
- a jug of water

The trick
1 Fold the cardboard in half.

2 Draw a large arrow on the cardboard (like the one shown in the picture).
3 Stand the cardboard on a table with the glass tumbler in front of it.

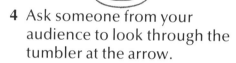

4 Ask someone from your audience to look through the tumbler at the arrow.
5 Fill the glass with water and the arrow will jump around to point in the opposite direction!

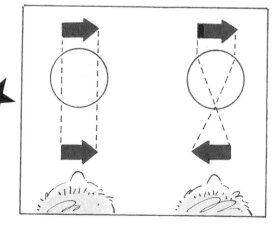

Magic Science
Pouring water into the glass causes the light rays from the arrow to bend, so it appears to turn around.

OBEDIENT BALL

A ping-pong ball rolls along a table by itself.

Apparatus
a comb
a ping-pong ball
woollen cloth (an old sweater
   would do)

The trick
1 Place the ball on a table.
2 Rub the comb vigorously with the wool.
3 Hold the comb near the ball.
4 The ball will roll towards the comb!

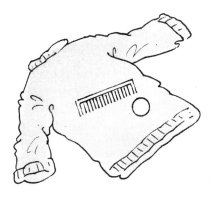

Magic Science
Everything we touch is made up of very tiny particles called *atoms*. Rubbing the comb causes the atoms to become charged with static electricity. It is this static electricity which attracts the ping-pong ball to the comb.

It's a fact
Our word "electricity" comes from "elektron", the Greek word for amber. When rubbed with fur, amber attracts dust and light things, such as feathers or bits of straw. This was first discovered by the Greek philosopher Thales of Miletus some 2,500 years ago! Many people used to believe that amber had magic powers.

WATER WIZARDRY

It's amazing! Turn a glass of water upside down – and the water will not fall out!

Apparatus

a glass of water
a piece of thin cardboard large enough to cover completely the rim of the glass

The trick

1 Place the cardboard on top of the glass of water.
2 Press your hand firmly on top of the cardboard.
3 With your hand still holding the cardboard in place, turn the glass of water over. Do this quickly and smoothly.
4 Slowly take your hand away from the cardboard.
5 Much to everyone's surprise, the cardboard remains in place and the water does not come out of the glass!
6 Hold the upside-down glass over a sink or bowl. Give it a shake, the cardboard will fall and the water will pour out of the glass!
7 Be careful to ensure that no air gets between the cardboard and the glass, or you are likely to receive quite a soaking!
8 Don't try this trick over your mother's best carpet – just in case anything goes wrong!

Magic Science

Although we don't normally notice it, air is pressing against everything. This force is called air pressure (see pp. 6, 15, 26, 27 & 44).

When the glass of water is held upside down the pressure of the water is pushing the cardboard away from the glass. At the same time, the air pressure is pushing up against the cardboard. Because the air pressure is greater than the water pressure the cardboard remains in place.

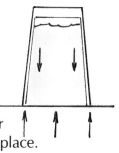

COIN IN MIND

A member of your audience is concentrating on one of two coins. You can tell her which coin she is thinking of!

Apparatus
two coins

The trick

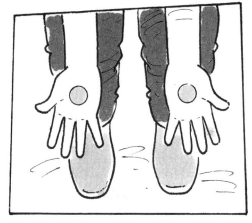

1 Ask someone from your audience to hold a coin in each hand and to place her hands on her knees.
2 Turn your back and ask her to think of either one of the coins.

3 Ask her to hold the hand containing the coin she has chosen up to her forehead.
4 Keep talking for at least twenty seconds. Ask her to concentrate on the coin.
5 Your friend then places her hand back on her knee.
6 You turn round and tell her which coin she chose.
7 All you have to do is take a quick look at her hands. The hand that is slightly lighter than the other will be the one holding the chosen coin.

Magic Science
As your friend holds her hand up to her forehead, blood drains out of that hand, which makes it paler than the other.

WHICH HAND?

Carefully choose a member of your audience. Hold his wrist and concentrate hard. You can tell him which hand he is thinking of.

Apparatus
one honest friend

The trick
1 Stand facing your friend.
2 Hold his left wrist with your right hand and his right wrist with your left hand.
3 With practice you will be able to place your hands so they can feel your friend's pulse in each wrist.
4 Ask him to think of one of his hands.
5 You will notice a slight slowing down and then a speeding up of the pulse of one hand. That is the hand your friend is thinking of. The pulse of the other hand will remain steady.
6 If you feel both pulses reacting it means that your friend cannot make up his mind which hand to choose!

LOOK SERIOUS AND TAKE YOUR TIME. YOUR AUDIENCE WILL REALLY BELIEVE YOU CAN READ MINDS.

Magic Science
When you concentrate on a particular part of the body the blood flow to that area increases. This increase in the blood flow makes the pulse beat faster.

IT'S A BREEZE

You make a soft breeze blow from your magic fingertips.

Apparatus
just yourself and a member of your audience

The trick
1 Tell your volunteer that you have magic fingers!
2 Ask her to hold one hand up with the palm pointing towards you.
3 Reach up into the air just above your head and pretend to catch something.
4 Tell your volunteer that you are trying to catch the wind.
5 Make another catch in the air.
6 Open your hand and bring it down flat towards your volunteer's hand.
7 Turn your hand sideways with your thumb on top as it gets alongside your volunteer's hand.
8 She will feel a breeze that appears to be coming from your fingertips.

Magic Science
As you bring your hand down you create a rush of air. Turning your hand at the last minute directs the breeze you have created towards your volunteer's hand.

EGG FLOAT

When you ask a member of your audience to put an egg into a jar of water it sinks to the bottom. When you put the egg into another jar it floats on the top. When you then put it into a third jar it floats halfway down!

42

Apparatus

an egg (hard-boiled is best, just in case you drop it!)
two small jars
one large jar
water
lots of salt
a spoon

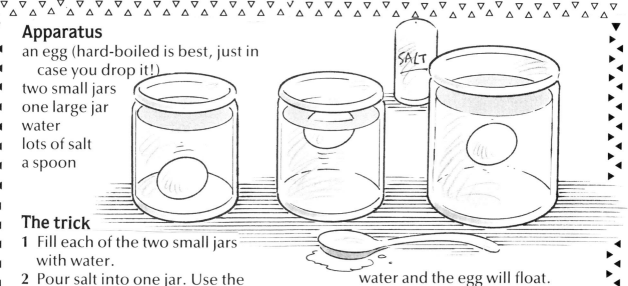

The trick

1 Fill each of the two small jars with water.
2 Pour salt into one jar. Use the spoon to stir and dissolve it.
3 Dissolve as much salt as you can. Make sure no one is watching!
4 Hand the egg and the jar of unsalted water to a volunteer from your audience.
5 Ask your volunteer to put the egg in the water (she can use the spoon to do this so that the water will not splash).
6 The egg will sink to the bottom of the jar.
7 Use the spoon to take the egg out of the water.
8 Put the egg into the salted water and the egg will float.
9 Remove the egg from the water.
10 Pour some of the salt water into the large jar.
11 Slowly and gently pour some of the ordinary water into the large jar.
12 Place the egg in the large jar and it will neither float nor sink but remain suspended part way in the water.
13 If you add more salt water the egg will move nearer to the surface.
14 If you add more ordinary water the egg will sink down again.

Salt water is more dense – that means it's thicker and heavier – than fresh water, so it supports the egg.

It's a fact

Have you ever noticed that it is easier to float in the sea than in a swimming pool? This is because of the salt in the sea water.

One sea, the Dead Sea, is so salty it is almost impossible to sink in it!

WHAT A BLOW

When you place a balloon over the neck of a bottle and ask someone from your audience to blow it up they just can't do it.

Apparatus
a balloon
a bottle

The trick
1 Dangle the balloon in the bottle and then stretch the neck of the balloon over the top of the bottle as shown in the picture.
2 Ask someone to try to blow the balloon up inside the bottle.
3 No matter how strong they are they will not be able to do it.

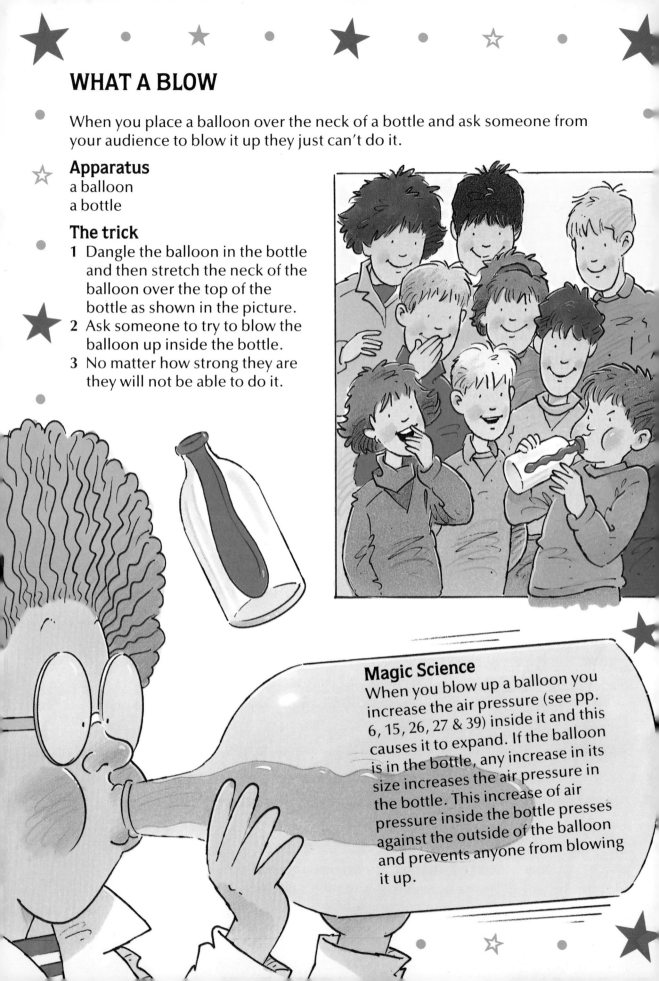

Magic Science
When you blow up a balloon you increase the air pressure (see pp. 6, 15, 26, 27 & 39) inside it and this causes it to expand. If the balloon is in the bottle, any increase in its size increases the air pressure in the bottle. This increase of air pressure inside the bottle presses against the outside of the balloon and prevents anyone from blowing it up.

THE BALLOON THAT GROWS

Now you can make a balloon blow up without puffing at all!

Apparatus
a balloon
a radiator

The trick

1 Blow some air into the balloon (not too much) and tie the neck.
2 Hold the balloon near a hot radiator as you command it to get bigger.

3 The balloon will start to grow. It must be magic!

Magic Science
The heat from the radiator warms the air inside the balloon. Warm air takes up more space than cold air, so the balloon gets bigger. Try not to make it obvious that you are holding the balloon near the radiator and the trick will appear to be real magic.

SECRET MESSAGES

And now for a little bit of mind reading. Ask a volunteer to do a simple sum. Magically the answer appears on a blank piece of paper!

Apparatus

a piece of paper
an old-fashioned pen nib (or a
    matchstick)
some milk
paper and a pencil for your friends

The trick

1 Dip the pen nib in the milk and use it to write the number 1089 on the piece of paper.
2 When the milk dries, the writing will be invisible. You are now ready to show the trick.

3 Show everyone the piece of paper. Mention the fact that there is nothing written on it.
4 Place the paper on a warm radiator or register. Tell your audience you have put it there so everyone can see that no one touches it.

5 Ask a volunteer to think of a three-digit number. Any number can be chosen but the three digits must all be different. The number can start or end with a zero, but always include the zero in your calculations.
6 Ask your volunteer to reverse the number.

7 Now ask her to subtract the smaller of the two numbers from the larger.

8 Now ask her to reverse the answer.

9 She must then add the first answer and the reversed answer together.

10 Ask your volunteer to call out the new total (it will be 1089).

11 Ask someone to show the piece of paper. Written on it is the number 1089!

Magic Science

The number will always be 1089. It works because of a simple mathematical trick. Follow the instructions given (and look at the example shown to make sure you understand it properly) and 1089 will always be the final answer.

Milk makes a good invisible ink. The heat from the radiator makes the writing visible. This is because different things burn at different temperatures. The radiator is not hot enough to burn the paper, but it is hot enough to burn the thin layer of milk that is on the paper.

LEMON JUICE MAKES GOOD INVISIBLE INK, TOO.

BAFFLING BOOMERANGS

Baffle your audience with these two boomerangs that seem to change their lengths.

Apparatus

the two boomerangs from the cardboard.
   section in the middle of this
   book

The trick

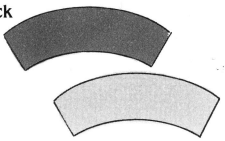

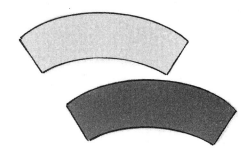

1 Hold the boomerangs with the red one above the other as shown. The red one looks shorter than the blue one.

2 Now hold them with the blue above the red. The blue boomerang now appears to be the shorter of the two.

Magic Science

Because the lower edge of each boomerang is shorter than the upper edge the brain is tricked into believing that the boomerangs are of different sizes.

THAT'S TORN IT

Challenge a volunteer to tear a piece of paper into three pieces. The paper will always end up in *two* pieces!

Apparatus

a piece of paper (about 10 cm × 20 cm)

The trick

1 Tear two slits in the paper as shown.
2 Ask your volunteer to hold one end of the paper in one hand and the other end in the other hand.
3 Now tell him to pull his hands apart and tear the paper into three pieces.
4 The paper will tear into two.

Magic Science

No matter how carefully the two slits are torn, one will always be slightly longer than the other. And, although paper looks flat and smooth, it is really quite bumpy. The lengths of the slits and the bumpiness of the paper mean that one slit will always tear through before the other.